The children were excited. They were going to
take part in a play. It was all about the history
of the town. The play was going to be held in the
park, and the children had to rehearse their
scene.

"I hope we don't forget what to do," said Chip.

Gran had come to watch the rehearsal.

"My goodness!" she said. "I don't believe it!
Biff is wearing a dress!"

"That's because we're children from World War
Two," said Biff. "Girls didn't wear trousers then."

"Our town was bombed in the war," said Chip.
"The bombing was called the Blitz."
Gran could remember it.

"I was only a girl," she said, "but I remember
the Blitz well."

"You wore awful clothes like these?" said Biff.

"We have to carry these boxes," said Wilma.
"But they are empty."

"They weren't empty in the war," said Gran.
"They had gas masks in them. We had to take
them to school every day."

"Gas masks?" gasped Wilf. "Fantastic!"

The children rehearsed their parts. In the play,
they were sent away to live in the country.
It wasn't safe to stay in the town because of the
bombing.

"We have to pretend to be upset," said Wilma.

Chip tried to pull a sad face.

"I'm going to pretend to cry," said Wilf.

He made a loud noise blowing his nose.

"Stop it," said Biff. "You're making me laugh."

The others began to laugh too.

"We shouldn't laugh," said Wilma.

Gran spoke to the children.

"The war was a terrible time for everyone," she said. "It wasn't funny."

"We're sorry, Gran," said Chip. "But it *was* a long time ago."

After the rehearsal, Wilf and Wilma went home
with Biff and Chip. Chip thought about the war.

"It must have been a hard time for children
then," he said.

"It's hard to imagine what it was like,"
said Wilf.

"I can't wait to take these clothes off," said
Biff. "I hate wearing this dress."
Suddenly the magic key began to glow. The magic
took the children off on another adventure. It took
them back to a street in London.

"We've come back to the war," gasped Chip.
"This looks like the scene in our play."
They saw a little boy all by himself.

"I was with my school," said the boy, "but I
got lost. May I come with you?"

Suddenly there was a long wailing sound.
"That's an air raid warning," said Wilma.
"It means we're going to be bombed."
People began to run. A man shouted at them.
"Hey!" he yelled. "Get into the shelter!"

Everyone went into the shelter. Above the
shelter, bombs were landing. Everything rocked
and shook.

"I'm scared," said the little boy.

"So are we," said Wilma.

"I hope it's safe down here," said Biff.

The noise went on for about twenty minutes.
Then it stopped. Everything was quiet for a little
while. Then the loud wailing noise began. The
air raid was over.

"That was really frightening," said Wilf.

The children came out of the shelter. They couldn't believe their eyes. The street had been bombed. There was smoke and dust everywhere. Wilma put her arm round the little boy.

One building was gone. It was just a pile of
bricks. Another building was on fire. Firemen were
starting to put the fire out.

"This is terrible," said Wilf. "I didn't think it
would be like this."

A woman ran up to the children. She took the
little boy's hand.

"Oh! I'm so glad I found you," she said.
She looked at the others.

"You must all have got lost, too," she said.
"Come on! The train will be leaving soon."

The station was crowded with children. They all had gas masks and they looked upset and unhappy.

"We are being sent away," said the little boy. "It's because of the bombing. It's too dangerous to live here."

A woman gave them all a brown paper bag.
Wilma looked inside hers.

"It's a dry old sandwich and an apple,"
she said, "but no sweets or chocolate bars."

"Of course not," said the woman. "What did
you expect?"

A man blew a whistle.

"Gas masks on," he ordered. "And don't worry, there is no gas. This is just a practice."

"We don't have gas masks," whispered Chip. "We only have empty boxes."

Wilf opened his box. Inside it was a gas mask.
They all had gas masks in their boxes.

"I can't believe it!" he gasped.

"Hurry up!" shouted the man crossly. "You
must put them on quickly."

Biff hated wearing the gas mask. It felt tight
and uncomfortable. It had a funny smell and it
felt hot. When she talked, her voice sounded
funny and the gas mask steamed up. She couldn't
wait to take it off.

"Ugh!" said Biff. "That was terrible. It was so
hard to breathe in that gas mask."
The man blew his whistle again. It was time to
get on the train. All the children had to line up.
The little boy began to cry.

"I don't want to go away," sniffed the boy.
"I don't even know where we are going."

"But it's not safe to stay," said Chip.

"My mum has to stay," said the boy.

Wilma gave the boy a packet of tissues.

"I've never seen tissues before," said the boy.

At last the train came in.

"It's a steam engine," said Wilf.
The train puffed out smoke and it made a
clanking noise. As it stopped, it gave a loud hiss.
Smoke and steam filled the air.

The grown-up began to call the children's
names out. Then they were told to get on the train.
"I don't think our names are going to be called
out," said Wilma. "They don't know who we are."

Wilma was right. The man came across to them.

"Why aren't you on the train?" he asked.

The woman looked at her list.

"There shouldn't be anyone left," she said.

"I don't know who these children are."

"We can't leave them behind," said the man.
"We can find out who they are later. But we'll
have to split them up."

"We don't want to be split up," said Biff.
"We want to stay together."

"I'm sorry," said the man. "I don't think
you can."

"We can't always keep children together,"
said the woman. "Not even brothers and sisters."
"That's terrible," said Chip.
Suddenly the magic key began to glow. The
adventure was over.

"I didn't like that adventure," said Chip.
"I was so scared being in that air raid."
"I felt sorry for the children," said Biff.
"Imagine having to leave home and going to
live with people you don't know."
"That poor little boy!" said Wilma.

Chip asked Gran to tell them about the war.
"I never saw a banana," said Gran. "There
wasn't much food. We didn't have lots of sweets or
chocolate. We didn't have nice soap and shampoo.
We only had a bath once a week."

It was the night of the play. Biff, Chip, Wilf and Wilma didn't laugh when they played their parts. They remembered the magic adventure. They thought of the children waiting for the train to come in.

Gran was pleased with them.

"You were really good," she said.

Biff told Gran a secret.

"The magic key showed us how hard it was in the war," she said. "I'm glad we only had to act it."